Alison Hawes

**Story illustrated by
Pet Gotohda**

Before Reading

Find out about

- Some inventions which started off big but got smaller and smaller

Tricky words

- mobile phones
- heavy
- smaller
- computers
- cameras
- minutes
- photo
- instantly

> Introduce these tricky words and help the reader when they come across them later!

Text starter

The first mobile phones were a good idea but they were big and heavy. So were the first computers, cameras and music players. But now they are much smaller.

What's the Big Idea?

Mobile phones

Mobile phones were a good idea.

But the first mobile phones were too big and heavy.

As mobile phones got smaller
and smaller, lots of people
wanted them.

Computers

The first computers were a good idea.
But they took up lots of room.

They looked like this.

As computers got smaller and smaller, lots of people wanted them.

Now a computer will fit in a pocket!

Now mobile phones can send emails!

Cameras

The first cameras were big and heavy.

They were a good idea.

But they took up to 15 minu
to take one photo!

Now a camera will fit in a pocket and it takes photos instantly!

Now many mobile phones are cameras as well.

Music players

The first music players were big and heavy.
They looked like this.

But music players got smaller and smaller.
Now lots of people have MP3 players.

They have a computer inside them to hold the music.

Quiz

11

Text Detective

- Why were the first cameras difficult to use?
- Which invention do you think is the best?

Word Detective

- **Phonic Focus:** Blending three phonemes
  Page 3: Can you sound out 'big'?
  What is the sound in the middle?
- Page 5: Find a word that means the opposite of 'bad'.
- Page 7: Find a word to rhyme with 'book'.

Super Speller

Read these words:

take   good   lots

Now try to spell them!

HA! HA! HA!

Q Why did the computer squeak?

A Somebody stepped on its mouse!

In this story

 Ag

Rocky

Tricky words

- fishing
- spear
- laughed
- idea
- catch
- pulled

 Introduce these tricky words and help the reader when they come across them later!

Story starter

Ag and her big brother Rocky are cave people who lived long ago. Ag is full of good ideas to make their lives more comfortable, but Rocky laughs at her ideas – he's so sure they will never catch on! One day, Ag and Rocky wanted to go fishing in the lake.

Ag
and the
Fishing Stick

Rocky wanted to go fishing in the lake.
So he got his big spear.

Ag wanted to go fishing too.
So she got her Fishing Stick.

"What is *that*?" laughed Rocky. "It's a Fishing Stick," said Ag.

"A Fishing Stick!" said Rocky. "What a silly idea!"

Do you think Ag's Fishing Stick is a silly idea?

15

Rocky got in the lake with his spear.

He got wet and he didn't catch a lot of fish.

Ag sat by the lake with her Fishing Stick.

She didn't get wet and she got a lot of fish!

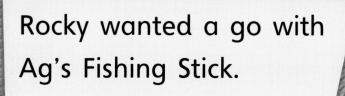

Rocky wanted a go with Ag's Fishing Stick.

"That Fishing Stick is a good idea," he said.

Do you think Rocky will catch lots of fish?

Ag let Rocky have a go with her Fishing Stick.

Rocky got a fish.
It was a **very** big fish.

It pulled Rocky in the lake!

Rocky got very wet and the big fish got away!

"I said that Fishing Stick was a silly idea!" said Rocky. "It will **never** catch on!"

Quiz

Text Detective

- How did Ag catch lots of fish?
- Why did Rocky say Fishing Sticks 'will never catch on'?

Word Detective

- **Phonic Focus:** Blending three phonemes
  Page 16: Can you sound out 'got'?
  What is the sound in the middle?
- Page 15: Find the word 'what' twice.
- Page 16: Find a word to rhyme with 'take'.

Super Speller

Read these words:

her   have   very

Now try to spell them!

HA! **HA! HA!**

 Q What do police fish ride in?

A Squid cars!

24